The Family Guide to

Thrive on a Dime

Smart Spending, Budget-Friendly Adventures, and Creating Lasting Memories on a Tight Budget

Copyright © 2024 by Clair Greenfield

All rights reserved.

ISBN: 9798304093651

No portion of this book may be reproduced in any form without written permission from the publisher or author,

except as permitted by U.S. copyright law.

Disclaimer: The information presented is purely to share our experience and for entertainment purposes. The author assumes no legal liability for the accuracy, completeness, or usefulness of any information, apparatus, product, or process disclosed in this book. The author disclaims liability for any damage, mishap, or injury that may occur from engaging in any activities or ideas from this book.

Table Of Contents

Introduction	4
Chapter 1: Embracing a Thrifty Mindset	6
Chapter 2: Budget-Friendly Travel Tips	10
Chapter 3: DIY Home Projects on a Budget	18
Chapter 4: Creative Meal Planning and Cooking	27
Chapter 5: Thrifting and Second-Hand Shopping Strategies	36
Chapter 6: Affordable Family Activities and Outings	44
Chapter 7: Smart Financial Planning for Families	53
Chapter 8: Frugal Parenting Tips and Tricks	61
Chapter 9: Low-Cost Hobbies for Families	68
Chapter 10: Building a Debt-Free Mindset and Lifestyle	80
Conclusion	89

Introduction

When I was growing up, my family lived on the edge of poverty. As an elder millennial born in the mid-1980s, I was homeschooled and raised on one income. We stretched every penny to make ends meet. Birthdays meant homemade cakes, and vacations were camping trips in the backyard. While we survived, it often felt like we were missing out.

Now, as a parent, I want something different for my family. I don't want to live in debt or waste money on unnecessary luxuries, but I also don't want to feel like we're just scraping by. That's where frugal living comes in. It's not about deprivation; it's about being smart. Frugality is the balance between saving money and enjoying life. This book is a practical guide to living well without overspending, so you can have the life you want while staying financially secure.

By adopting this approach, you can create a lifestyle that's not just about cutting costs but about finding joy in resourcefulness. Whether it's crafting your own holiday traditions, discovering new hobbies that don't cost a fortune, or teaching your kids the value of a dollar, frugal living is empowering. It allows you to reclaim control over your finances while still making room for meaningful experiences and adventures.

Chapter 1: Embracing a Thrifty Mindset

The Benefits of Frugal Living

Living with intention can totally turn things around for your family—not just your bank account, but how you enjoy life together. If you're dealing with tight budgets or drowning in debt, it's time to shake things up. The good news? You don't have to live like a monk to make it work. It's about focusing on what really matters: connection, creativity, and having fun without spending a fortune.

Let's start with travel. You don't need to book fancy flights or five-star hotels to have amazing adventures. Road trips are underrated—crank up the music, pack some snacks, and hit the open road. Or pitch a tent at a national park and roast marshmallows under the stars. Even exploring local spots during off-peak times can feel like a mini-vacation. The best part? These trips aren't just easy on your wallet—they're packed with memories your kids will talk about for years.

At home, why not turn saving money into a family project? DIY is where it's at! Got an old chair collecting dust? Give it a makeover together. Want cool wall art? Grab some paint and let the kids unleash their inner artists. Not only will you save cash, but you'll also make your space uniquely yours. Plus, working together on projects like this is a great way to bond (and sneak in a few lessons about patience and teamwork).

Now, food—who doesn't love food? Instead of blowing your budget on takeout, try cooking at home as a family. Get the kids involved in chopping veggies or stirring sauces. You'll save money, eat healthier, and maybe even discover a new favorite dish. Bonus points if you meal prep for the week—it's like a gift to your future self when life gets busy.

And when it comes to family fun, don't underestimate the power of free stuff. Parks, library events, community festivals—they're everywhere, and they're awesome. You don't have to spend big to have a great time. In fact, these little adventures often bring the most laughter and the best memories.

Making intentional choices isn't about giving things up—it's about finding smarter, more meaningful ways to live. When you work together as a family, you don't just save money; you build something way more valuable: a life full of joy, connection, and purpose.

Shifting Your Family's Perspective on Money

Changing how your family thinks about money starts with open, honest conversations. If financial stress feels like a constant weight, it's time to reframe how you see money. Instead of viewing it as a source of worry, think of it as a tool for reaching your goals. Talk about it as a family—share thoughts, feelings, and even frustrations. These discussions are a chance for parents to model healthy attitudes while helping kids understand that money isn't just about earning and spending—it's about making smart choices. When kids learn early that money is a tool, they grow up feeling more confident and capable.

Next, get everyone involved in budgeting. Create a family budget together and make it interactive. Use charts, apps, or even stickers to track expenses. Let the kids help decide where the money goes—should you save up for a day trip, a new board game, or a movie night? Celebrate wins like staying on budget or scoring discounts at the grocery store. These little victories show that working as a team pays off (literally!) and make managing money feel like a group effort instead of a chore.

Meal planning can also completely change how your family sees spending. Instead of dreading grocery shopping, turn it into a fun challenge. Plan meals together, look for recipes using affordable seasonal ingredients, and see who can come up with the best ideas for saving money. Maybe it's a contest to cook dinner for under $10 or finding creative ways to use leftovers. Not only does this teach resourcefulness, but it also shows that cooking on a budget can be fun—and delicious.

Thrifting is another great way to shift your family's mindset. Who doesn't love the thrill of finding a hidden gem? Turn trips to thrift stores, garage sales, or flea markets into treasure hunts. Make a game out of it—find the best deal, the coolest vintage item, or something to upcycle into a family project. When kids see that second-hand shopping is more about adventure than settling for less, they'll learn to value the hunt and the savings.

Finally, build a debt-free mindset as a family by setting achievable goals. Talk about the importance of living within your means and saving for things you truly care about. Create a family savings jar and decide together what you're working toward—maybe a vacation, a special treat, or even just a fun outing. Watching the jar fill up turns saving into a shared experience, and reaching your goal feels like a win for everyone.

When you approach money as something to work with—not against—you teach your family to see its potential. With these simple shifts, you'll create a healthier, happier relationship with money that sets everyone up for success down the road.

Chapter 2: Budget-Friendly Travel Tips

Planning Affordable Family Vacations

Planning a budget-friendly family vacation can be just as exciting as the trip itself. With a little creativity, you can craft unforgettable adventures without draining your savings. Start by getting the whole family involved. Gather around the table, share ideas, and dream up destinations together. When everyone has a say, the trip becomes more than just a getaway—it feels like a shared goal that you're all working toward.

Timing is everything when it comes to affordable travel. Off-peak seasons are a goldmine for deals on hotels, attractions, and flights. Plus, smaller crowds mean more space to enjoy yourselves. Look into local festivals or events happening during your trip—many offer free or low-cost activities that can add something special to your itinerary. By staying flexible with your dates, you'll open up opportunities to save big while still having a blast.

Accommodations don't have to eat up your budget. Home exchanges are a great way to skip hotel costs and experience life like a local. Vacation rental platforms often have affordable options, especially if you book early or choose less touristy areas. Or, why not try camping? It's an adventure on its own—roasting marshmallows, sleeping under the stars, and waking up to nature. Many parks offer budget-friendly camping sites that are perfect for families.

Food is another area where you can save without sacrificing fun. Bring along snacks and simple meals for road trips or day outings to avoid pricey convenience store stops. If you're staying somewhere with a kitchen, plan a few meals to cook together as a family. Trying local ingredients and whipping up something new can be a highlight of the trip—not just a way to save. And for dining out, keep an eye out for family specials or kids-eat-free nights.

The real magic of any vacation isn't in how much you spend—it's in the moments you share. Explore free attractions like parks, trails, or museums on free-admission days. Create a scavenger hunt to turn sightseeing into a game. Community events can also be hidden gems, offering entertainment and a chance to soak up local culture.

When you focus on experiences rather than expenses, every outing feels like an adventure. These vacations aren't just easier on your wallet—they're packed with memories that will stay with your family forever. By embracing simple joys and working together, you can turn any trip into something truly special.

Finding Cheap Accommodations

Finding affordable accommodations for a family trip can feel like a fun treasure hunt —especially when you know where to look. Start by diving into budget travel websites and apps. They're packed with deals, from vacation rentals to family-friendly hostels. Make sure to compare prices across platforms and read reviews to avoid surprises. With a bit of digging, you'll discover unique stays that fit your budget and create lasting memories.

Think outside the tourist hotspots. Staying in suburban or rural areas often comes with cheaper rates and an authentic glimpse into local life. Bonus: many places outside the city center offer perks like kitchens or laundry facilities. Cooking a few meals or tackling laundry mid-trip can stretch your budget even further. These small savings can add up, giving you more room to splurge on activities or souvenirs.

Loyalty programs and off-peak travel are other game-changers. Many hotel chains offer rewards like free nights or discounted stays, so signing up can really pay off. Traveling outside the busy seasons can also land you incredible savings—not to mention quieter attractions. Less crowds and lower rates? That's a win-win!

For a truly unique experience, consider house swapping. There are websites that connect families who are willing to trade homes for a set time. It's a fantastic way to save on lodging while living like a local. Imagine staying in a cozy home, complete with a stocked kitchen and backyard, while your kids get a glimpse of how other families live. It's a budget-friendly option with an extra dose of adventure.

Don't forget about your personal network. Sometimes, friends or family might have vacation homes or know someone willing to rent out a place at a discount. A quick post on social media or a conversation with a neighbor could lead to unexpected options. It's amazing what a little community networking can uncover.

With some creativity and teamwork, finding budget-friendly accommodations can become one of the highlights of your travel planning. Plus, it's a great way to teach your kids the value of smart choices—while still making incredible memories together.

Navigating Transportation on a Budget

Navigating transportation on a budget can feel like a fun family challenge, with plenty of creative ways to save while keeping your adventures rolling. Whether it's a cross-country road trip or just a run to the store, small tweaks can make a big difference. Start with a plan: map out your routes and combine errands to cut down on unnecessary trips. Fuel-saving apps can help you track down the cheapest gas stations, while traffic apps keep you out of frustrating delays that waste both time and gas.

Public transportation is another smart option that turns travel into an adventure. Many cities offer discounted family passes, making buses, trains, and trams a cost-effective way to explore. Your kids might even find the ride itself exciting—bonus points if the route takes you somewhere new! Check for free or discounted days at museums, parks, or other attractions accessible by public transit. It's an easy way to save while teaching your kids how valuable and fun community resources can be.

And don't forget the simplest option: your own two feet (or a pair of wheels). Walking and biking are not only budget-friendly but also healthy and eco-friendly. Turn these outings into family adventures by planning a scavenger hunt or exploring local trails. It's a great way to make the journey just as exciting as the destination.

By getting creative with transportation and involving the whole family in the process, you'll save money, reduce stress, and teach your kids how to navigate life resourcefully. Plus, you'll make plenty of memories along the way—proof that even getting from point A to point B can be part of the adventure!

Free and Low-Cost Activities at Your Destination

Exploring new destinations doesn't have to be expensive—there are so many free and low-cost activities that can turn any trip into a memorable adventure. With a bit of planning and a focus on the experiences that don't come with a hefty price tag, your family can enjoy everything a place has to offer without feeling the stress of spending too much. Local parks, community events, cultural festivals, and free museum days are just the start.

By embracing these wallet-friendly options, you'll discover that some of the best memories come at little to no cost.

First, check out the local community calendar to find free events happening during your stay. Many cities host outdoor movies, concerts, and seasonal festivals—great opportunities for families to enjoy the sights and sounds of the area without spending a cent. These events are often packed with fun activities for kids, food trucks, and local artisans, creating a lively atmosphere that brings everyone together. It's also a fantastic chance for your kids to meet new friends and for you to immerse yourselves in the local culture.

Don't forget to take advantage of the natural beauty of the area! Parks, beaches, and hiking trails often offer free access to breathtaking landscapes. Pack a picnic and spend the day exploring nature, or plan a family adventure with a scavenger hunt or nature bingo to keep the kids engaged. Whether you're hiking through the woods or just enjoying a stroll along the beach, these outdoor activities are not only cost-effective but also provide a healthy, active way to bond as a family.

If you're in a city, consider free walking tours or exploring on your own. Many cities have rich histories and fascinating stories that can make any neighborhood a living museum. Download free podcasts or use apps to turn your walk into an educational experience. You might find hidden gems and learn cool facts about the area—plus, it's a great way to stay active and explore at your own pace. Don't forget to snap photos to capture these moments for your travel memories!

Finally, think about DIY activities that add a special touch to your trip without costing extra. Encourage your kids to keep a travel journal or create a scrapbook with souvenirs and notes from the trip. This helps them reflect on the experience and sparks their creativity. You can even recreate the places you visit at home by hosting themed dinners based on the food you tried on your trip. It's a fun way to keep the adventure alive long after the vacation ends.

By thinking outside the box and embracing budget-friendly options, you can make every trip an enriching experience that's just as much about the journey as it is about the destination. With a little creativity, you'll find that the best adventures are often the ones you least expect!

Chapter 3: DIY Home Projects on a Budget

Simple Home Improvements for Less

Simple home improvements can make a big difference in your living space without costing a lot of money. For families on a budget, the key is to focus on projects that are affordable but impactful. Start by looking around your home for small changes that could have a big effect. A fresh coat of paint can completely transform a room, and choosing a soft, neutral color can make the space feel bigger and more peaceful. This is a project the whole family can get involved with, turning it into a fun bonding experience that's finished in just a weekend.

Decluttering and organizing is another great way to improve your home without spending much. Not only will your space look better, but it will also be more practical. Get the kids involved by sorting through toys, clothes, or items they no longer need. You can donate or sell things, turning clutter into cash. Look for affordable storage solutions at thrift stores or online marketplaces to help keep everything organized. It's a great way to teach your children the value of organization and generosity.

Adding some greenery to your home with indoor plants can also make a big difference. Houseplants can brighten up a room and even improve air quality. You don't need to spend a lot—many plants can be grown from cuttings or found at local nurseries or swaps with friends. Involving your kids in caring for the plants teaches them responsibility and lets them connect with nature. Plus, watching the plants grow is a rewarding experience for everyone.

Updating small fixtures around the house is an easy way to give your space a fresh look. Replacing old doorknobs, cabinet handles, or light fixtures can make a noticeable difference. These items are often available at second-hand stores or online for a fraction of the price. Even just cleaning or polishing what you already have can restore its shine and appeal. This is a great chance to involve your kids in a hands-on project and teach them some basic home maintenance skills.

Lastly, think about creating a family space that encourages togetherness without spending a lot. Rearranging furniture can give a room a new feel without any extra cost. Set up a cozy reading nook with pillows and blankets, or create a game area with a second-hand table and chairs. Get everyone involved in choosing the layout and decor, which will encourage teamwork and creativity. These small changes can create a warm, welcoming atmosphere in your home, where everyone can make lasting memories without the need for expensive upgrades. Embrace these simple home improvements to make your home more inviting and functional while sticking to your budget.

Creative Upcycling Ideas

Creative upcycling is a fun and smart way for families to turn everyday items into something new and useful, all while sticking to a budget. Instead of throwing away old furniture or household items that have seen better days, think about how you can give them a second life. For example, an old wooden ladder can be transformed into a charming bookshelf or a unique plant stand with a little paint and creativity. Not only does this save money, but it also brings the family together as you work on projects that might otherwise end up in the trash.

One simple upcycling project is turning glass jars into beautiful storage solutions. These jars can be used to organize craft supplies, pantry items, or even serve as decorative vases. A coat of paint or some twine can turn them into eye-catching decor for any room. This project is great for kids because it lets them express their creativity while learning about recycling and reusing. Plus, it helps declutter your home without spending a cent.

Another great upcycling idea is giving worn-out clothing a new purpose. Instead of throwing away that favorite shirt with a small stain, consider turning it into a reusable tote bag. Simply cut off the sleeves, sew the bottom shut, and you've got a stylish, eco-friendly bag for grocery shopping or outings. This is a fun, hands-on project to do with kids, and it teaches them the importance of resourcefulness and sustainability—valuable lessons for a frugal lifestyle.

Furniture upcycling can be an exciting way to refresh your home on a budget. Take an old coffee table and paint it in bright colors or add a mosaic of tiles to the top for a fresh look. This not only breathes new life into your home, but it also serves as a great conversation piece. Involving the whole family in these projects encourages teamwork and creativity, making it a rewarding experience for everyone involved.

Don't forget about the kitchen when thinking about upcycling. Old kitchen utensils can be turned into charming wall art, or mismatched plates can be used to create a unique serving display. These projects help showcase your family's personality and creativity while keeping costs low. Upcycling is more than just saving money; it's about embracing creativity and sustainability, making it a perfect fit for families who want to live a fulfilling and budget-conscious lifestyle.

Budget-Friendly Decor Tips

Transforming your home into a cozy and stylish space doesn't have to cost a lot. With a bit of creativity and resourcefulness, you can refresh your space without spending a fortune. One of the easiest ways to start is by repurposing items you already own. Take a look around your home for furniture or decor that could serve a new purpose. For example, an old ladder can be turned into a charming bookshelf, or mismatched chairs can be painted the same color for a unified look. By thinking outside the box, you'll save money and create one-of-a-kind pieces that showcase your family's style.

Thrifting is another great way to find budget-friendly decor. Local thrift stores and flea markets are full of hidden treasures just waiting to be found. Look for decor, artwork, or even furniture that can be easily updated with a coat of paint or a little cleaning. Don't shy away from items that seem outdated—a vintage piece can bring character to your home when styled properly. Plus, the hunt for a great find can turn shopping into a fun family outing, with kids getting involved in the process of finding something special.

DIY projects are another wonderful way to spruce up your home while spending time with your family. Get your kids involved in simple crafts that can enhance your space. Whether it's painting flower pots or creating wall art from recycled materials, these projects help teach kids new skills while encouraging their creativity. Dedicate a weekend to a family home improvement day, where everyone pitches in to make your space feel more inviting. Not only does this create lasting memories, but it also instills a sense of pride in your home.

Seasonal decor is also an affordable way to refresh your home's look. By switching out decorations for different seasons or holidays, you can keep things fresh without spending extra money. Use natural elements like pinecones, leaves, or flowers to create seasonal centerpieces or wreaths. This not only makes your home feel festive, but it also provides a fun way to teach your children about the changing seasons. Plus, it's a great way to bond over crafting and nature walks.

Lastly, don't underestimate the power of decluttering. Reducing the number of items in your home can make it feel larger and more organized. Get the whole family involved by sorting through your belongings together and deciding what to keep, donate, or sell. This helps clear out unnecessary clutter while giving everyone a sense of accomplishment. You'll be surprised at how a simpler, more organized space can elevate your home's overall look, all without spending a dime. Embrace these budget-friendly decor ideas and watch your home transform into a stylish, welcoming space that reflects your family's personality!

Organizing Your Space Without Breaking the Bank

Transforming your home into a well-organized, peaceful space doesn't have to cost a fortune or require a professional organizer. With a little creativity and some teamwork, you can make your home a clutter-free haven on a budget. Start by gathering the family for a fun weekend project to sort through your living areas. Make it a game to decide what you truly need and what could be donated or repurposed. This not only helps you declutter but also teaches everyone the value of letting go of things that no longer serve a purpose, creating a calmer environment for everyone.

Next, take a good look around your home to see how you can use what you already have for storage. Old crates, baskets, or even suitcases can easily be turned into stylish and functional storage solutions. Think vertically, too! Adding a few shelves can free up floor space and keep things organized. If you're feeling crafty, try turning an old wooden pallet into a rustic shelf or shoe rack. These DIY projects are not only budget-friendly but also give your home a personalized touch that reflects your family's unique style.

Thrifting is another fun and affordable way to find storage solutions. Many thrift stores are packed with hidden gems just waiting to be discovered. You might find vintage baskets, decorative boxes, or even pieces of furniture that just need a little love, like a fresh coat of paint or new fabric. Get your kids involved in the process—turning it into a family adventure where everyone helps find the perfect pieces to organize and beautify your space.

Don't forget about your kitchen! Organizing your kitchen can be a game-changer for meal prep and reducing clutter. Set up a designated spot for meal planning and keep things neat by using clear containers for ingredients. Not only does this make cooking easier, but it also helps cut down on food waste—saving money and helping your family eat healthier. Get the kids involved in planning meals for the week, teaching them important life skills while keeping everything in order.

Remember, organizing your home is a journey, not a race. Set a small budget each month to slowly build up your organizational tools and solutions, and celebrate your progress along the way. Maybe it's hosting a family movie night in your newly organized living room or simply enjoying a cozy evening in your decluttered space. By taking it one step at a time, staying within budget, and involving the whole family, you'll create an organized, stylish home that reflects your family's personality—and teach valuable lessons about teamwork and creativity along the way

Chapter 4: Creative Meal Planning and Cooking

Planning Weekly Meals on a Budget

Planning meals on a budget doesn't have to feel like a chore—it can be a fun family activity that saves money and brings everyone together in the kitchen! With a little creativity and a bit of organization, you can turn meal planning into something your whole family will look forward to. Start by involving your kids in the process. Let them help brainstorm ideas for meals and pick out recipes they're excited to try. Not only does this give them a sense of ownership, but it also encourages them to try new foods they might not have otherwise considered.

To get started, take stock of what you already have in your pantry and fridge. You might be surprised by the ingredients you already have that can be turned into delicious meals. Once you've gathered everything up, create a meal plan around those ingredients. Choose versatile foods that can be used in several dishes throughout the week. For example, a big bag of rice can be the base for stir-fries, casseroles, or even rice salads, making it a budget-friendly staple.

When you're ready to make your grocery list, keep an eye on sales and seasonal produce. Farmers' markets and weekly sales are great places to find fresh fruits and vegetables at lower prices. By building meals around what's in season or on sale, you can save money while making your meals even more flavorful and nutritious. Also, consider buying in bulk for pantry staples like pasta, beans, and grains. These items are often cheaper when bought in larger quantities and can last for weeks.

Another great way to save time and money is by embracing batch cooking. Set aside a few hours on the weekend to prepare big batches of meals you can freeze or store in the fridge for later. Soups, stews, and casseroles work really well for this and make busy weeknights much easier. Plus, getting the family involved in the cooking process can be a great bonding experience, with everyone pitching in to create something tasty that you can all enjoy together.

Finally, don't be afraid to get a little adventurous! Cooking on a budget doesn't mean your meals have to be boring. Make it fun by having themed nights where you explore different cuisines or try recreating your favorite takeout dishes at home. Not only does this add some excitement to your meals, but it also teaches everyone valuable cooking skills while helping to broaden your palates. The key is to make lasting memories and build healthy habits that will benefit your family for years to come, all while staying within your budget. Happy cooking!

Smart Grocery Shopping Strategies

Smart grocery shopping is one of those everyday skills that can really help families stretch their budgets while still enjoying healthy, delicious meals. With just a few simple strategies, you can make the most of every grocery trip, filling your pantry without draining your wallet. Start by creating a thoughtful shopping list based on your planned meals for the week. This helps you avoid those tempting impulse buys and ensures you only pick up what you actually need. It also helps reduce food waste! To make it even more fun, involve your kids in the meal planning. They'll love having a say in what's on the table, and it's a great way to teach them about budgeting.

One of the best ways to save is by taking advantage of sales and discounts. Keep an eye out for local store flyers or download grocery store apps that alert you to weekly deals. Stocking up on pantry staples, like rice or canned goods, during a sale is a smart way to save money over time. If you find a great deal, consider buying in bulk, but only if it fits within your budget and storage space.

And don't forget about coupons! It might seem old-school, but many stores still accept them, and there are lots of websites and apps that make it easy to find and organize coupons for you.

Shopping seasonally is another wonderful way to save. When produce is in season, it's often much cheaper and tastier. Plan your meals around in-season fruits and veggies to get the most bang for your buck. If you have a local farmers' market, it's a great place to find fresh produce at lower prices, and sometimes even organic options at a fraction of the cost. Plus, supporting local farmers and teaching your kids about the seasons can be a fun way to build healthy eating habits together.

Don't forget to check out the less popular aisles in the store, too! Frozen fruits and veggies, for example, can be a more affordable option compared to fresh, but still offer great nutritional benefits and last longer. You can also save by trying store brands or generic products. They often cost less than name brands but don't compromise on quality. Encourage your family to try these alternatives, and you may find some new favorite products that are both budget-friendly and tasty!

Lastly, online shopping and delivery services can be a big help, especially if you can find discounts or free delivery offers. Shopping online lets you stick to your list (and avoid the temptation of impulse buys!) while saving time. If you're worried about delivery fees, look for stores that offer free delivery on your first order or for purchases over a certain amount.

Ultimately, smart grocery shopping is about being proactive, creative, and involving your whole family. With these simple tips, you'll turn grocery shopping into a fun, budget-friendly family activity that keeps everyone healthy and happy!

Cooking with Leftovers: Waste Not, Want Not

Cooking with leftovers is a wonderful way to save time and money while getting creative in the kitchen! When you embrace the idea of "waste not, want not," you're not only keeping your grocery bills in check, but you're also opening the door to all kinds of delicious, budget-friendly meals. Think of it as a fun challenge—how can you take what's left from last night's dinner and turn it into something exciting today?

The first step is to plan your meals around what you already have. This means thinking ahead while you cook. For example, if you roast a chicken for dinner, consider how the leftover meat could be used in a fresh chicken salad, a flavorful stir-fry, or a comforting soup. By making a little extra on purpose, you can set yourself up for another tasty meal without extra effort. Not only does this reduce food waste, but it also helps you get more out of your grocery budget, stretching those dollars a little further.

Involve your kids in this creative process! Turn leftover night into a fun family activity where everyone pitches in with ideas. You could even set up a "leftover buffet" where each family member can create their own dish from what's available. It's a great way to encourage your kids to be adventurous eaters, while also teaching them the value of being resourceful in the kitchen. Plus, it's a perfect opportunity to show them how to store and reheat leftovers safely—a valuable skill for the future.

And don't forget the magic of sauces and spices! A simple homemade sauce can completely transform the flavor of a dish. For example, take those leftover veggies, sauté them with garlic and olive oil, and toss them with pasta and your favorite sauce for a quick and delicious weeknight meal. Or use some seasoning to turn bland rice into savory fried rice. These small changes can make your leftovers feel brand new, so everyone in the family will look forward to eating them again.

To keep everything organized, consider creating a leftover inventory. Stick a simple list on your fridge to remind you of what you have on hand. That way, you can easily incorporate those ingredients into your meal planning for the week. Staying organized will help you avoid the "what's for dinner?" dilemma and make sure you're using what you already have, reducing food waste.

Cooking with leftovers isn't just about saving money—it's a chance to get creative, teach your family important skills, and make the most out of what's in your kitchen. So, roll up your sleeves, and let's have some fun with those leftovers! You might be surprised at how many tasty meals you can make.

Family-Friendly Recipes That Save Money

Cooking for your family on a budget doesn't have to be overwhelming—it can actually be a great adventure! The key is to get a little creative in the kitchen and make smart choices that keep your grocery bill low, all while serving up delicious and nutritious meals. Start by stocking up on affordable and versatile staples like beans, rice, and seasonal vegetables. These ingredients are the backbone of so many meals and can stretch your budget while keeping everyone full and satisfied.

One of the easiest ways to save is by planning meals around sales and what's in season. Check out your local grocery store's weekly flyer and plan your family's meals based on the discounted items. Not only will this save you money, but it'll also encourage you to try new ingredients or recipes that you might not have considered before. Who knows—you might just discover a new family favorite! You can also make meal prep a breeze by batch cooking on the weekends.

Cooking in larger quantities and freezing portions for later means you'll have quick, homemade meals ready for busy nights, cutting down on last-minute takeout costs.

Make meal prep a family affair! Involve your kids in the cooking process by letting them help with tasks like measuring ingredients or chopping veggies. This not only makes cooking fun, but it's also a great way to teach them the value of budgeting and where food comes from. Why not create a "family recipe night" where everyone comes up with a dish using affordable ingredients? It's a fun, hands-on way to encourage teamwork, creativity, and a little friendly competition in the kitchen.

Embracing frugal cooking isn't just about saving money—it's about creating memories, bonding with your family, and teaching valuable skills. With a little planning and creativity, you can make meals everyone will love, all while sticking to your budget.

Chapter 5: Thrifting and Second-Hand Shopping Strategies

Finding Hidden Gems at Thrift Stores

Thrift stores are like hidden treasures just waiting to be discovered, and for families looking to save while adding some fun and flair to their lives, they can be a real goldmine! The excitement of finding something unique is like a mini adventure every time you step inside. From vintage clothing to quirky home decor or even toys for the kids, thrift stores are full of possibilities that can help stretch your budget and bring a little extra character to your home and wardrobe. So why not embrace the hunt and let your creativity lead the way?

To make the most of your thrift store visits, try exploring a few different locations in your area. Each one has its own collection of items, and you never know what hidden gems you might find. Why not turn it into a fun family outing? Make it a scavenger hunt where everyone gets to help find things on your list—or even better, let the kids explore and come up with their own ideas for unique finds. Not only does this make shopping exciting, but it also teaches them the value of resourcefulness and reusing items instead of always buying new.

It's easy to feel a little overwhelmed when you walk into a thrift store, especially with so much to choose from. So, it helps to have a clear idea of what you're looking for. Are you on the hunt for a new set of dishes, a stack of books for family reading night, or maybe some art supplies for your next DIY project? Having a focus will help you sift through all the items with purpose. And remember, thinking outside the box can lead to some wonderful surprises—a vintage suitcase could become a stylish side table, or an old picture frame could be the perfect base for a family photo collage.

When you're making your thrift store rounds, timing is key. Many stores restock on certain days, so if you can find out when those are, you'll have an edge on the best finds! Early visits can often lead to the most exciting discoveries. Keep an eye on seasonal sales too, as many stores offer discounts or special days with everything marked down. Being flexible with your schedule and checking in regularly can lead to incredible savings, especially when you're able to find the perfect pieces at a fraction of the cost.

And once you've found your treasures, why not celebrate? Share your amazing finds with your family and turn it into a tradition. Whether it's showing off a DIY project you've completed or a unique outfit you've put together, it's a great way to teach the value of creativity and being thrifty. Encouraging your kids to be proud of their finds will help them develop lasting habits of frugality and resourcefulness.

So grab your shopping bags and head to your local thrift store! It's a fun and rewarding experience that will enrich your family's life without breaking the bank. Enjoy the adventure and the treasures you uncover along the way!

Tips for Successful Garage Sales and Flea Markets

Shopping at garage sales and flea markets can be a fantastic way to score unique finds while sticking to a budget. It's like a treasure hunt, where the thrill of the search is just as fun as discovering a hidden gem! With a little creativity and a bit of strategy, you can make the most of your shopping trips while saving money and adding something special to your home or wardrobe.

Start by making a list of what you're hoping to find, whether it's clothing, home decor, or toys for the kids. Having a general idea of what you're looking for helps you stay focused and makes the shopping experience less overwhelming. But leave a little room for surprises—you never know what might catch your eye! Involving your kids in the process is a great way to make it an exciting family outing. Turn it into a scavenger hunt where they can help look for specific items, or just let them explore and find something that sparks their imagination. Not only will it be fun, but it teaches them the value of reusing and repurposing items.

One of the best parts of garage sales and flea markets is the potential to haggle a little. While you don't want to be pushy, don't be afraid to ask for a better price, especially if you're buying multiple items. Many sellers are open to negotiating, and it can be a great learning opportunity for your kids about the value of money and respectful bargaining. For instance, if you spot a bundle of books or a few pieces of decor, ask if the seller can offer a discount for purchasing several items together—it's a win-win for both you and the seller!

When shopping, keep an open mind about the condition of items. Some pieces may need a little TLC, but that's where your creativity comes in! A worn piece of furniture can be repainted and given a new life, or an old picture frame can be turned into a stylish chalkboard. Look for potential and don't be afraid to see things through a different lens. This approach not only stretches your budget but also gives you the chance to personalize and get crafty with your finds.

Timing can also make a big difference when hunting for deals. Some flea markets or garage sales offer discounts later in the day, especially if they're eager to clear out remaining items. If you're willing to shop a little later, you might score some great last-minute bargains. On the flip side, the best stuff often sells fast, so if you have a particular item in mind, getting there early can help you snag it before someone else does.

Finally, make your shopping trip a fun experience by creating a little tradition. After each outing, celebrate your family's finds together—whether it's a new toy for the kids, a vintage jacket for yourself, or a quirky home accent for your living room. Discuss what you've discovered and how you plan to give your treasures a new home. This helps reinforce the idea that second-hand shopping isn't just about saving money—it's about finding something special, while being kind to the planet and supporting local sellers. Happy hunting!

Online Shopping for Second-Hand Deals

Online shopping for second-hand deals has turned into an exciting treasure hunt for families looking to save money without sacrificing quality. Whether it's gently used clothing, toys, or household items, the digital marketplace is full of opportunities to find great deals. Not only will this help you stick to your budget, but it also supports sustainable living, which is a win for both your wallet and the planet!

A great place to start your online second-hand shopping adventure is with dedicated platforms and apps. Websites like eBay, Poshmark, and Facebook Marketplace are fantastic for finding used items. They're user-friendly and let you filter your search by size, condition, or even brand, so you can easily track down exactly what you're looking for. The best part? You can shop from home, making it easy to squeeze into your busy day.

Don't forget about local community groups on social media! Many neighborhoods have groups for buying, selling, and swapping items, where you can find amazing deals on things like children's clothes, toys, and furniture—all at a fraction of the price you'd pay in stores. Plus, you can often arrange for local pick-up, saving on shipping costs and giving you a chance to see the item in person before committing. It's a great way to support your community while keeping your spending in check.

Patience is key when it comes to online second-hand shopping. Unlike new retail items that are stocked regularly, second-hand treasures can be a bit unpredictable. Make it a habit to check your favorite platforms frequently, and set alerts for the items you're after. Sometimes, the thrill of the hunt is half the fun! With a little persistence and a sharp eye, you might score an unbelievable deal at just the right moment.

While shopping, remember to keep your budget in mind. It's easy to get excited about finding great deals, but setting a spending limit will help keep you from making impulse purchases. Make a list of what your family truly needs or wants before diving in—it will guide you toward smart, purposeful buys that really benefit your household. With a bit of creativity, patience, and resourcefulness, you can enjoy the adventure of second-hand shopping while making sure your family enjoys fulfilling and affordable finds.

Teaching Kids the Value of Thrift

Teaching kids the value of thrift is such an important life lesson that can set them up for responsible money habits and a more sustainable lifestyle. By introducing this mindset early on, you can help your children learn the joy of living within their means—especially in families where budgets are tight. Rather than seeing thriftiness as something restrictive, you can turn it into a fun and creative adventure. This not only encourages responsible spending but also brings the family closer together through shared experiences.

One fun and hands-on way to teach thrift is through meal planning and cooking. Get your kids involved in choosing recipes that use affordable, nutritious ingredients. You can have family cooking nights where everyone pitches in to turn simple ingredients into a tasty dinner. Let them help plan meals based on what's on sale or what you already have in the pantry. Not only does this teach them cooking skills, but it also helps them appreciate how planning ahead can save money and reduce food waste.

Another great way to introduce the concept of thrift is by exploring second-hand shopping together. Make a trip to local thrift stores or flea markets into a treasure hunt. Talk about how valuable items can often be found for a fraction of the cost of new ones, and encourage your kids to hunt for specific things or put together creative outfits using second-hand finds. Not only will this show them how to save money, but it also teaches them the environmental benefits of reusing and recycling. The excitement of finding hidden gems will foster a lifelong love for thrifty shopping!

There are also plenty of affordable family activities that can teach thriftiness in a fun way. Look for free or low-cost events in your community, such as park visits, nature hikes, or free workshops. You can even create your own family traditions like picnics or game nights at home. Ask your kids to suggest ideas for fun, budget-friendly outings, which will help them feel empowered while reinforcing the idea that great experiences don't have to come with a big price tag. This encourages creativity and shows that happiness can often be found in the simplest, most affordable activities.

Helping your kids develop a debt-free mindset is another key part of teaching them the value of thrift. Talk as a family about saving for special things, like a vacation or a big purchase. You can use visual tools, like a savings chart or jars for different goals, to make the idea of saving tangible. Discuss the difference between needs and wants, and why it's important to stick to a budget. Involving them in these conversations will give them the tools to make smart financial decisions as they grow, while also instilling pride in living a thrifty, debt-free life.

By turning thrift into a family adventure, you're setting your kids up for success— teaching them creativity, resourcefulness, and the power of thoughtful spending.

Chapter 6: Affordable Family Activities and Outings

Fun at Home: Budget-Friendly Family Nights

Family nights at home are a wonderful way to connect and make memories without spending a lot. Designate one night a week for family fun—whether it's game night, movie night, or a themed dinner. By making it a regular tradition, everyone will look forward to it! Use what you already have around the house to set the mood, like string lights or homemade decorations, and the excitement of the evening will feel extra special.

Games can bring so much joy to these nights. Dig out those old board games or make your own using everyday items. Charades is a fun and easy option, or you could create a scavenger hunt around the house. If you have a deck of cards, try a new card game, or get the family involved in a jigsaw puzzle. The key is to have fun together while fostering teamwork and communication.

Movie nights are another great option. Browse your streaming services or check out your local library for DVDs to make sure everyone can enjoy a movie night without spending a dime. Make it extra cozy with some homemade popcorn and encourage everyone to bring their favorite blanket or pillow. You could even make it a themed night—perhaps a classic movie marathon or animated favorites. Let the kids help choose the movie, then chat about it afterward to spark some fun conversation and critical thinking.

Cooking together is another way to bond while staying within your budget. Choose a theme for dinner—maybe Italian or Mexican—and let everyone pitch in by making a dish. Cooking as a team teaches kids valuable skills and brings everyone together in the kitchen. If you have picky eaters, involve them in the menu planning so they'll be more excited about what's on the table. It's also a great time to discuss budgeting and cooking with what you have in the pantry.

You could also host a family talent show to tap into everyone's creativity. Let each family member showcase something they enjoy—whether it's a song, a funny skit, or a magic trick. The kids can even create their own short plays or skits to perform. Not only does this get everyone laughing, but it also boosts their confidence and encourages them to share their talents. And don't forget to capture these moments in a family scrapbook with photos and stories to look back on.

Family nights like these help create lasting memories, strengthen your bond, and nurture creativity—all while being easy on the budget. They're a perfect way to enjoy each other's company and make the most of time spent together.

Exploring Nature: Free Outdoor Activities

Spending time in nature is a great way for families to connect, learn, and have fun without needing to spend much. The outdoors offers plenty of free activities that promote health, create lasting memories, and allow you to enjoy quality time together. Whether it's a walk through the woods or spotting local wildlife, nature has something for everyone. These experiences also provide an opportunity to introduce your kids to the beauty of the environment while strengthening your family bond.

Hiking is one of the easiest and most rewarding ways to enjoy the outdoors. Many local parks offer trails that are perfect for all skill levels, so the whole family can join in. Pack a picnic, put on your walking shoes, and head out on an adventure. Along the way, take time to observe the surroundings and talk about the plants and animals you encounter. Bring along a notebook or sketchpad for the kids to capture their favorite sights—whether through drawing or writing. It's a fun mix of exercise, creativity, and exploration.

Visiting local beaches, lakes, or rivers can also provide hours of enjoyment. These natural spots are often free to access and offer activities like swimming, fishing, or building sandcastles. Whether you're casting a line or working together to make the best sand sculpture, these activities promote teamwork and creativity. Remember to bring sunscreen, snacks, and plenty of water to keep everyone hydrated and safe while enjoying the sun.

Community gardens and parks are also great places to connect with nature. Many local gardens welcome families to volunteer, learn about gardening, and even take home fresh produce. It's an excellent way to teach kids about healthy eating and sustainability. Also, many parks host free events, such as outdoor movie nights or concerts. Keep an eye on local listings to find events near you that the whole family can enjoy.

For something interactive, try organizing a nature scavenger hunt. Whether you're in a city park, a wooded area, or even your own backyard, this activity can be tailored to your surroundings. Create a list of things for the kids to find—different types of leaves, rocks, or even birds—and see who can check off the most items. It's a fun way to get everyone moving while sparking curiosity and teamwork. Plus, the excitement of finding each item will make the experience memorable.

Nature is full of simple adventures that help create lasting memories, all while staying budget-friendly. These activities can bring your family closer together and inspire a lifelong love for the outdoors.

Community Events and Free Festivals

Community events and free festivals are an amazing way for families to have fun, make memories, and enjoy each other's company—without spending a ton of money. Whether it's live music, art exhibits, or food tastings, there's always something new to explore. Many of these local events celebrate the community's culture, history, and traditions, giving your family a chance to learn while having a great time together. These outings are a great way to bond and spark new interests in your kids.

The best part? These events are usually designed to be fun for everyone. Kids can enjoy face painting, games, and bounce houses while you relax and take in the scene. It's a fantastic way for families to spend quality time together, without the pressure of spending money. And when everyone's enjoying themselves, you're teaching your kids the value of community and creativity—lessons that will stick with them long after the event is over.

Don't forget, these events also showcase local talent, from live performances to art displays. This can be a great way for your kids to see how others express themselves and maybe even get inspired to try something new. Whether it's drawing, playing an instrument, or trying out a new craft, these events can spark creativity and open up new hobbies for your family to explore together.

Involving your kids in the planning can also be a fun way to teach them about budgeting. Instead of spending money on big outings, why not make it a habit to check out free events happening nearby? Let your kids help you pick out the events they're excited about. This not only gets them excited about the plans but also teaches them the value of researching and making decisions. Plus, it's a great opportunity to bond while staying on track with your budget.

And, who knows? You might meet other families at these events who share similar goals and interests. You could swap tips for budget-friendly activities, or even come up with fun ideas for future gatherings. By getting involved in your community, you're creating lasting memories while building a supportive network of like-minded families.

So, the next time there's a local festival or community event, grab your family, check it out, and enjoy all the free fun. It's a great way to learn, laugh, and connect—all without spending a thing!

Creative Playdates That Don't Cost a Pretty Penny

Creative playdates are a fantastic way for kids to bond, have fun, and get their imaginations flowing—all without breaking the bank. The best part is that these playdates don't need to be fancy or expensive. By thinking outside the box and using the resources around you, you can create memorable experiences that your kids will love, without spending a lot of money.

One of the easiest and most fun ideas is to take advantage of the great outdoors. A nature scavenger hunt in a local park is a perfect way to get kids excited about exploring. Make a list of things for them to find—like acorns, feathers, or different kinds of leaves—and watch their faces light up as they search for these treasures. It's not just about finding the items, though; it's also a chance for kids to learn about nature, work together, and enjoy being outside. Pack some simple snacks and a picnic blanket, and you've turned a regular day into an adventure.

When the weather isn't great for outdoor fun, hosting a DIY craft party at home is a great alternative. You don't need to buy expensive supplies—use what you already have around the house! Old magazines, scrap paper, pasta, and even cardboard boxes can become the building blocks for fun, creative projects. Let the kids' imaginations run wild as they make their own creations. At the end, host an art show where everyone can share their masterpiece. It's a wonderful way to boost their creativity and make them feel like true artists.

If you want to add some learning to the mix, why not try a themed storytime? Invite a few other parents and kids to bring their favorite books for a cozy reading session. Pick a fun theme, like animals or adventures, and have everyone dress up according to the theme. It's a great way to inspire a love of reading while adding a bit of imagination to the mix. You can even follow up with a related craft or discussion, making it a fun and educational experience for everyone.

Lastly, don't underestimate the power of classic games. A backyard Olympics can be a blast for kids of all ages. Think simple activities like sack races, three-legged races, or tug-of-war. You don't need anything fancy—just a little space and some energy! It's a great way to keep kids active and teach them teamwork, all while having a ton of fun.

With these easy, creative ideas, you can host playdates that your kids will remember, and you won't need to spend a lot to make it happen. By using what you have and tapping into your kids' creativity, you'll be able to create experiences that bring joy, encourage learning, and keep your budget intact.

Chapter 7: Smart Financial Planning for Families

Creating and Sticking to a Family Budget

Creating a family budget is one of the best ways to take charge of your finances and feel more in control of your money. It can seem overwhelming, especially if you're on a tight budget or dealing with debt, but it's a great step toward financial stability. To get started, gather all the information about your income, monthly bills, and any debts. This will help you see exactly where your money is going and give you a clear picture of your finances. Once you know this, you can find areas where you can cut back or make smarter choices to meet your family's needs and goals.

Involving your family in the budgeting process is a great way to teach kids valuable lessons about money. It also helps everyone feel like they're working toward the same goals. Sit down together and talk about your family's financial goals. Whether it's saving for a vacation, paying off debt, or cutting back on spending, having a shared vision makes everyone more accountable. You can use simple tools like budgeting apps or a spreadsheet to track your progress. Make it a family project—this way, budgeting feels more like a fun challenge than a boring task.

As you work on your budget, it's important to focus on what you need versus what you want. This doesn't mean you have to cut out fun completely—it's about being smart with your money. You can still enjoy family outings by looking for affordable ways to have fun, like traveling during off-peak times or finding discounts for activities. Consider DIY projects at home that can make your space feel fresh without spending a lot. By finding creative ways to enjoy life affordably, you'll get the most out of your budget and make memories that last.

Meal planning is another great way to keep your budget in check. Take time each week to plan meals that are healthy and cost-effective. You can create a shopping list based on what's on sale or what you already have at home, so you don't waste money on unnecessary items. Get your kids involved in meal prep to teach them about cooking and nutrition while also giving them a sense of accomplishment. Not only does this help save money, but it also turns mealtime into an enjoyable family activity.

It's also important to check in on your budget every few months. Life changes, and your financial needs will too. Sit down with your family regularly to go over how things are going, celebrate your wins, and figure out what needs to change. The goal is to create healthy, sustainable habits that help you live within your means and teach your kids lifelong money skills. By embracing the journey of frugal living, you'll feel more financially secure and better prepared for whatever comes next.

Saving for the Future: Setting Goals

Saving for the future is an important skill for families, especially when you're working with a limited income or managing debt. The good news is that setting clear, realistic goals can make all the difference. It can turn saving into something exciting rather than stressful, and it helps you make the most of what you have. Start by thinking about what you really want to achieve. Maybe it's a family vacation, home improvements, or a college fund for your kids. When you know what you're working toward, it becomes easier to focus your efforts and get excited about the process.

Once you have your goals in mind, it's time to prioritize them. What matters most to your family? Maybe a summer trip is a bigger priority than buying a new appliance, or perhaps paying for your kids' education should come before upgrading your car. By ranking your goals, you'll know where to focus your energy and money. This helps keep everyone motivated and makes budgeting easier, because you'll be clear about what you need to save for first.

Now, let's break those big goals down into smaller steps. Big goals can feel overwhelming, but when you take them one step at a time, they're much more manageable. For example, if your goal is a family vacation, figure out how much you need to save each month. Then, think of little ways to cut back and save, like planning meals ahead to lower your grocery costs or finding free activities in your community. These small steps can add up over time, and the whole family can feel proud of the progress.

Including your kids in the saving process can also help them understand the value of money and the importance of saving. Talk to them about why you're saving and involve them in setting goals. Whether it's helping out with chores or setting aside part of their allowance, they'll feel more connected to the goal. You can even create a family savings jar to visually track your progress. It makes saving fun and shows them that everyone plays a part in reaching the goal together.

Finally, remember to celebrate your wins, big or small. Whether you reach a savings milestone or finish a DIY project on a budget, take the time to appreciate your hard work. Celebrating these moments can keep your family motivated and make saving feel more rewarding. By making saving a fun, shared experience, you'll not only improve your financial situation, but you'll also create lasting memories and strengthen your family bonds.

Understanding Credit and Debt Management

Understanding credit and managing debt is an important skill for families, especially when you're working with a budget but still want to enjoy life's little adventures. Whether you're on a tighter income or trying to get on top of debt, learning how credit works and finding ways to manage your debt can set your family up for a brighter future. This way, you can still plan fun vacations, tackle DIY projects at home, or enjoy outings without the weight of financial stress hanging over you.

Credit can be a helpful tool when used wisely. It allows you to make bigger purchases, like a car or home, that might be out of reach if you were saving for them alone. But it's important to understand how your credit score affects your ability to borrow money. A higher score can help you get better interest rates, which means you'll pay less in the long run. It's a good idea to check your credit report regularly to make sure everything looks right. Keeping an eye on it can help you make smarter choices and stay on top of your finances.

When it comes to managing debt, the key is to have a plan that works for you and your family's needs. Start by making a list of all your debts—what you owe, the interest rates, and when payments are due. This will help you see clearly which debts to focus on first. You might choose to use the snowball method (paying off the smallest debt first for a quick win) or the avalanche method (tackling the high-interest debt to save money in the long run). Having a clear plan can help you stay motivated and feel good about the progress you're making.

Being creative and frugal can also help you pay down debt faster. Plan meals around affordable ingredients and cook more at home to save money on groceries. Thrift shopping for clothes and household items is another great way to keep expenses down. Look for free or low-cost activities to enjoy as a family—whether it's hiking, having a game night, or exploring local parks. When frugality becomes a family activity, it not only helps you manage debt but also teaches your kids valuable lessons about managing money.

Building a debt-free lifestyle is about more than just numbers; it's about creating a mindset that values resilience and creativity. Make talking about money a normal part of family conversations. Celebrate your wins, big or small, like paying off a credit card or hitting a savings goal. These celebrations can keep your family motivated and focused on your financial journey. When you understand credit and manage debt well, you'll feel empowered to live life to the fullest while staying financially stable.

Teaching Kids About Money

Teaching kids about money is one of the best ways to set them up for a successful future, especially for families who are working with a tighter budget. Helping children understand how money works, the importance of saving, and how to manage their expenses can make a big difference in their ability to make smart financial choices as they grow.

Start by talking about money during everyday activities. When you take trips to thrift stores or visit budget-friendly markets, use those moments to show how you can find good deals without overspending. Explain how you budget for these outings and let your kids know that having fun doesn't always require spending a lot. These simple lessons help kids see money management as something practical and positive, rather than stressful.

Make learning about money fun by turning it into games at home. You can set up a pretend store with play money where kids can practice buying things. This helps them understand the difference between what they want and what they need. Encourage your kids to set small savings goals—whether it's for a toy or a treat—and help them track their progress. Watching their savings grow will make them excited about learning to manage their money.

Another way to teach your kids about money is by including them in family budgeting. Explain how you decide how to spend money on groceries, bills, and savings. Use simple words and create a budget chart that everyone can help fill in. This visual approach helps kids see where the money goes and how saving can lead to something fun, like a family outing or a special treat. By involving them in these decisions, you show them that budgeting is a family effort.

It's also helpful to teach your kids the importance of living within your means. Talk about debt and why it's better to avoid it. Share real-life examples, like why your family chooses to shop secondhand instead of buying new. Show how doing things creatively, like taking on DIY projects at home, can be a way to save and still enjoy life. These lessons help kids see being careful with money as a good habit that gives them more freedom in the future.

Finally, encourage your kids to try activities that are both fun and teach important life skills. Cooking together is a great way to save money while learning about nutrition and meal planning. Gardening can teach patience and responsibility, as they take care of their plants and watch them grow. These activities are a great way to spend time together while learning valuable lessons about money, all without breaking the bank.

Chapter 8: Frugal Parenting Tips and Tricks

Cost-Effective Childcare Solutions

Teaching kids about money is one of the best ways to set them up for a successful future. This is especially important for families who might be working with a tighter budget. By helping children understand how money works, the value of saving, and the basics of budgeting, you can give them the tools to make smart financial decisions later on.

Start by bringing up the idea of money in everyday situations. Family trips to thrift stores or affordable markets are great chances to show how you can get good value without overspending. Talk about how you budget for these outings and explain that having fun doesn't always have to come with a big price tag. These moments help kids see that money management isn't something to be afraid of, but something that can be done with simple choices.

You can also turn learning about money into fun activities at home. Try making a game out of saving and spending. Set up a pretend store where kids can use play money to buy items, helping them learn about transactions and the difference between wants and needs. Encourage them to set a savings goal, whether it's for a small toy or a special treat. Help them track how close they are to reaching their goal.

This hands-on approach makes learning fun and gives kids a sense of accomplishment as they work toward something they want.

Involving your kids in family budgeting can also be a great way to teach financial lessons. Explain how you make decisions about where the money goes, like paying for groceries, bills, or savings. Use simple words and let them help create a budget chart. This gives them a visual of where money is spent and helps them understand how saving can lead to rewards, like a fun family trip or a special treat. It also teaches them that budgeting is something the whole family does together.

It's important to help your kids develop a mindset that values living within your means. Talk to them about the idea of debt and why it's better to avoid it. Share simple examples, like why your family chooses to buy secondhand items instead of new ones. Highlight how creativity, like doing DIY projects at home, can save money and still bring joy. By focusing on positive choices like these, kids will see frugality as something empowering, not something to be ashamed of.

Lastly, help your kids discover hobbies that are both fun and teach them useful life skills. Cooking meals together is a great way to save money and also learn about nutrition and planning. Gardening can teach patience and the value of hard work, as kids watch their efforts grow into something rewarding. These activities are not only great ways to bond, but they also help kids understand how to manage money while creating lasting memories. A frugal lifestyle can be filled with creative, fun, and meaningful experiences!

Thrifty Birthday Party Ideas

Throwing a fun birthday party on a budget is totally possible! With a little creativity and some smart planning, you can create a celebration your child will love and remember—without spending too much. It all starts with choosing a theme that excites your child. Whether it's superheroes, princesses, or their favorite TV show, a theme can help guide your decorations, games, and activities. Look for themed items at local thrift stores, or use things you already have at home to make decorations. Remember, it's about creating a fun vibe, not about having fancy, expensive items.

Food is another area where you can keep costs low. Instead of buying an expensive store-bought cake, why not bake one together with your child? Let them help with decorating, which can be a fun part of the celebration. For snacks, go with simple finger foods like mini sandwiches, popcorn, or fruit skewers. You could even ask your guests to bring a dish to share, turning the party into a potluck. Not only does this make it more affordable, but it also adds variety to the menu and gives everyone a chance to contribute something special.

When it comes to games and activities, you don't need to spend a lot to keep kids entertained. Set up a DIY craft station using supplies you already have, or organize classic outdoor games like sack races, tug-of-war, or a scavenger hunt at a local park. If you're feeling artsy, you could host a painting party where each child makes their own masterpiece to take home. The goal is to make the day fun for everyone, not to have a competition, so everyone feels included and celebrated.

Invitations don't have to cost a lot either. Instead of buying fancy cards, try sending digital invitations or make your own using recycled paper and craft supplies. It's a great way to get your kids involved in the planning, and homemade invites can feel extra special. Plus, going digital saves on postage and paper!

And remember, the best part of any birthday party is the memories made. Instead of focusing on big, expensive gifts, encourage guests to bring something simple, like a favorite book or a small handmade gift. This teaches kids the joy of giving and sharing, while keeping costs low. Be sure to take lots of photos during the party, and maybe even create a scrapbook together afterward. Planning a memorable, budget-friendly birthday can be a fun way to bond with your family and show your kids how creativity and thoughtful planning can make any celebration special.

Affordable Education Resources

Finding affordable education resources can make a world of difference for families who want to enrich their kids' learning without overspending. While quality education can often come with a high price, there are plenty of budget-friendly options available that provide meaningful learning experiences. From online resources to community programs, there are many ways to help your children grow, all while sticking to your budget.

One of the best (and easiest) ways to access free education is through online resources. Websites like Khan Academy, Coursera, and YouTube are packed with free tutorials and courses on subjects like math, science, art, and even coding. These platforms let your kids learn at their own pace and explore topics they're curious about. Incorporating these into your family's routine is a great way to encourage learning outside the classroom while keeping things fun and affordable.

Don't forget about your local library! Libraries are an amazing (and often overlooked) resource. Beyond just borrowing books, many libraries offer free programs, events, and workshops for kids and families. Whether it's storytime, STEM activities, or arts and crafts, these programs can make learning fun and social. Plus, most libraries provide free access to online learning tools and e-books, giving your kids even more ways to explore and learn from home.

Community organizations and non-profits are also fantastic places to find free or low-cost educational opportunities. Many local groups offer tutoring, classes, and enrichment programs that help your children develop new skills and make friends. These programs are a great way to give your child extra academic help or introduce them to something new, all while saving money.

Lastly, don't forget that learning can happen just about anywhere! Family trips to museums on free admission days, nature hikes, or even cooking dinner together can provide rich learning experiences. Everyday moments are filled with chances to teach kids about the world around them. Embracing these opportunities can help make learning a natural part of your family's day, without adding extra costs.

By being resourceful and creative, you can give your children a well-rounded education that prepares them for the future, all while staying within your budget. It's all about using the tools and opportunities around you to make learning enjoyable, exciting, and affordable!

Fun and Free Family Traditions

Creating fun family traditions doesn't have to be expensive or complicated! Some of the best memories are made from simple activities that bring everyone together. Let's dive into a few ideas that are easy, affordable, and most importantly, full of fun!

How about starting a weekly game night? You don't need fancy games to have a blast—just use the ones you already have at home. Or even better, create your own! Get creative with things around the house to make new games, and watch as everyone enjoys some friendly competition. It's a perfect way to bond and share lots of laughs, all without spending a penny.

Another great tradition could be having a monthly "Cultural Night" where your family explores a different country. Pick a place you're curious about, and learn together. You can cook a simple dish, watch a movie, or try to learn a few words in a new language. Use your local library or free online resources to bring the culture to life. It's an exciting way to travel without leaving home!

Nature is a wonderful, cost-free playground! Set up a weekly family nature walk or hike in a local park or nature reserve. Pack a picnic with leftovers, and encourage your kids to collect leaves, rocks, or flowers along the way. At home, you can turn their finds into a creative scrapbook. Not only does this get everyone outside and moving, but it also nurtures a love for the environment.

Crafting together can also be a fun way to spend time. Grab some old magazines, cardboard, or leftover fabric, and let your imagination run wild. Whether you're making gifts, decorations, or just fun art projects, crafting helps everyone express their creativity. Plus, you get to proudly display your family's work around the house.

Another idea that's simple and meaningful is starting a family book club. Choose a book everyone can enjoy, then gather around to talk about it. You can enjoy snacks you made together while discussing characters, themes, and what you all learned. It's a great way to encourage reading and spark interesting conversations while making memories.

With these easy and affordable traditions, you can build a lifetime of memories without spending much at all. The best part? The love, laughter, and connection you create together will mean the most!

Chapter 9: Low-Cost Hobbies for Families

Discovering Free or Low-Cost Activities

Creating fun family moments without spending a ton of money is easier than you think! There's a whole world of exciting and free or low-cost activities right at your fingertips. You don't need big plans or a huge budget to make lasting memories; sometimes, the best moments happen when you get a little creative and embrace what's around you. Here are some ideas to help you get started!

Why not dive into what's happening around your community? Many towns host free events, like outdoor concerts, local festivals, or even farmers' markets. These are perfect opportunities for a family outing. You get to explore, enjoy local food, and support your neighborhood, all without spending much. And don't forget about your local library! Libraries offer free programs that are perfect for kids and families—story time, movie nights, arts and crafts, and even workshops. They're an awesome, often-overlooked resource that can provide hours of entertainment.

If you're looking to get outside, the possibilities are endless. Whether it's a walk in a nearby park, a hike on a local trail, or even a trip to the beach, nature offers tons of free fun. Pack a picnic, bring some games, and let your kids enjoy exploring the world around them. Gardening can also be a great family activity—planting flowers, veggies, or herbs together. It's a wonderful way to teach kids patience while creating something beautiful as a team.

Looking for ways to tap into your creative side? DIY crafts are always a hit! Take a look around your home for supplies—old magazines, cardboard, leftover fabric, or buttons—and get busy creating something together. Whether it's homemade cards, fun art projects, or even a family-made board game, crafting is a fantastic way to bond. Plus, it's a fun, budget-friendly way to make something special that you can all enjoy and be proud of.

Another easy and fun activity is cooking together. You can have a "family cook-off" or just pick a recipe that everyone can help with. Not only does this teach kids about cooking and nutrition, but it also makes for a fun and delicious family event. You could even turn it into a learning experience by experimenting with new recipes that are both healthy and affordable.

And if you're looking to add something new to your family's routine, consider picking up a hobby together. From painting to photography to simple science experiments, there are so many online resources that offer free lessons. You don't need fancy equipment—just a little imagination and a willingness to try something new as a family!

At the end of the day, it's not about how much money you spend, but the memories you make. Whether you're exploring the outdoors, getting creative with DIY crafts, or cooking a new meal together, the time you spend as a family is priceless. So, get out there and enjoy the simple, fun things life has to offer!

Engaging in Arts and Crafts on a Budget

Arts and crafts are an amazing way to bring your family together, spark creativity, and have fun—all while keeping things budget-friendly. The best part? You don't need fancy supplies to get started! With just a bit of imagination and a few everyday items, you can create beautiful projects that everyone will enjoy.

Start by looking around your home for materials you already have. Old newspapers, empty boxes, fabric scraps, and even plastic containers can be turned into something amazing. You can encourage your kids to get involved by letting them gather up things they no longer use, showing them how even "junk" can have new life with a little creativity. Not only does this help you save money, but it also teaches kids the value of recycling and reusing.

If you're ready to shop for more supplies, local thrift stores and dollar stores can be treasure hunts for crafting materials. Paint, brushes, beads, and even canvases can often be found for a fraction of what they cost at bigger stores. Set a small budget and take your kids along to find the supplies you need—this turns shopping into a fun adventure and teaches kids how to make thoughtful choices within a budget. You could even make a "crafting kit" with everything you buy, then see where your kids' creativity takes them with the new materials.

Another great way to find crafting inspiration is through online tutorials. There are endless websites and social media pages filled with step-by-step ideas that use minimal supplies, perfect for a family craft day. If you're lucky, your local library or community center might offer free craft workshops too! These are a great way to learn new skills while connecting with other families. The best part? They often have materials you can use, so it's totally free.

Seasonal crafts are also a fun way to create family memories while staying on budget. For example, in the fall, you could gather leaves to make colorful collages, or in winter, you could create homemade holiday decorations using things you find around the house or in nature. Crafting for holidays isn't just a creative outlet—it also gives you a chance to talk about family traditions and values, helping everyone feel more connected.

Why not turn crafting into a friendly family challenge? Pick a theme or project, then give each family member a set budget to work with. Once everyone's finished, you can host your very own "family art show" and admire each other's creations. This not only encourages everyone to think outside the box but also brings plenty of laughs as you see how each person interprets the challenge.

By making arts and crafts a regular family activity, you'll create an environment where creativity and resourcefulness thrive. Plus, you'll be teaching your kids that you don't need to spend a lot to have a good time together. So grab some supplies, get your hands a little messy, and let the fun begin!

Exploring Sports and Fitness Without the Price Tag

Getting active as a family doesn't have to cost a fortune! In fact, staying fit and having fun together can be both exciting and affordable. While some people think the only way to be healthy is by signing up for a pricey gym membership or sports program, there are so many ways to stay active without spending a lot. With a little creativity and a sense of adventure, you can discover fitness opportunities right in your neighborhood or even in your own backyard.

One of the easiest and most enjoyable ways to get moving is by spending time outdoors. Local parks, playgrounds, and walking trails are free and offer plenty of space for activities. Organize a family game of soccer, frisbee, or tag, and get everyone involved—kids will love burning off energy while parents can join in too. Nature walks, bike rides, or simply going on a stroll around the neighborhood are also fun ways to stay active while enjoying the outdoors. Remember, the best part about these activities isn't the price tag—it's the time spent together!

For families who enjoy more structured activities, local community centers are a goldmine for affordable fitness options. Many offer free or low-cost classes like yoga, Zumba, or dance, which are perfect for all ages. Don't forget to check out your library too! Some libraries offer fitness workshops or even free DVDs and online resources to help you set up a home workout routine. These opportunities make staying active easy and give you the chance to connect with others in your community.

If you prefer to create your own fitness fun at home, why not set up a DIY sports day? You can build an obstacle course in your backyard, or make sports equipment from things you already have around the house. For example, old socks can turn into soft "balls," or you can use cones made from recycled bottles. This adds a creative twist to fitness and teaches your kids about resourcefulness while keeping them active.

Another great way to keep fitness a part of family life is by making it a routine. Instead of sitting down to screen time after dinner, why not go for a family walk or turn on some music and have a living room dance party? The goal is to make exercise a regular and enjoyable part of your daily life, which helps build healthy habits for everyone in the family. And the best part? You don't need to spend anything to make it happen!

Staying fit as a family is all about creativity and making the most of the resources you already have. By exploring these fun and affordable options, you can keep everyone moving and having a blast, without breaking the bank. So gather your family, get active, and enjoy the journey to a healthier lifestyle!

Finding Joy in Nature and Outdoor Adventures

Getting outdoors and enjoying nature as a family is one of the best ways to connect and create lasting memories, and it doesn't have to cost anything! Whether it's a park down the street or a nature trail a little further out, the great outdoors has so many amazing adventures waiting for you. No need for fancy trips—just a little imagination and a love for exploring!

Start by checking out the local parks near you. Many of them have playgrounds, picnic areas, and open spaces for playing games. You can make a day of it by packing a simple lunch and enjoying some time together in the fresh air. For an added adventure, why not plan a scavenger hunt? You can make a list of things like finding a pinecone, a bright leaf, or a smooth rock, and send the kids on a treasure hunt! This is a fun way to get everyone moving and learning about the environment, all while making awesome memories.

If you're in the mood for something a bit more adventurous, consider a family hiking trip. Many nature trails are free to explore and offer stunning views, wildlife, and a chance to stretch your legs. Pack some snacks, lace up your shoes, and hit the trails together. It's a great way to exercise, learn about nature, and just enjoy each other's company. You can even make a game out of spotting different animals or identifying plants along the way.

Check out local outdoor events too—many communities host free or low-cost festivals, art fairs, or nature walks. These are perfect for getting out of the house, exploring something new, and meeting other families. Be sure to watch for these events on social media or community bulletin boards. It's a fun, easy way to enjoy family time and learn new things.

And don't forget, you can also try nature-inspired hobbies that are easy and fun for everyone. You could start a small garden in your backyard, get into birdwatching, or even just spend some time stargazing on a clear night. These activities don't require much, but they're so enriching. Plus, they give your family plenty of opportunities to bond, create, and learn together.

Nature has so much to offer—whether you're taking a walk, having a picnic, or just sitting under the stars, there's always something to discover. Best of all, it's all free! So grab your family, get outside, and see what kind of adventures you can have without spending a dime. You'll be surprised at how much fun you can have just by stepping out your door!

Chapter 10: Building a Debt-Free Mindset and Lifestyle

Understanding the Importance of Being Debt-Free

Living debt-free is like unlocking a whole new world of possibilities for your family, especially if you're working with a tight budget. It might feel tough at first, but the rewards of living without the weight of debt can be life-changing. When you're not constantly worried about monthly bills or paying off loans, you can focus on what truly matters: making memories, enjoying time together, and living with less stress. Imagine being able to make decisions based on what makes you happy, not what's required to keep up with payments. That shift can help you embrace a more fulfilling lifestyle that's full of joy and creativity.

One of the best parts about being debt-free is that it gives you the freedom to enjoy more budget-friendly adventures. Without the pressure of bills, you can put money toward fun experiences like weekend getaways or camping trips. You don't need to spend a fortune to have an amazing time. Sometimes the best family memories come from simple things, like exploring a local park or hiking a nearby trail. These outings can strengthen family bonds and bring everyone closer together without the stress of money hanging over you.

Living debt-free also inspires you to get creative with everyday tasks, like home projects. Whether it's painting a room, building your own furniture, or making decorations, working on DIY projects together is a great way to save money and teach valuable skills. Plus, there's something so rewarding about completing a project as a team. It makes your home feel even more like a special place where everyone contributes, and the pride you feel from a job well done is priceless.

When it comes to meals, a debt-free mindset can turn grocery shopping into a fun, creative challenge. Planning meals together and finding ways to make healthy, delicious dishes on a budget can be a bonding experience in itself. Let your kids pitch in by helping you plan meals, chop ingredients, or set the table. They'll learn important life skills and, even better, they'll get excited about the idea of eating better and wasting less. Plus, being mindful of your grocery budget means you can spend more on the things that matter—like those family adventures you've been dreaming of!

And don't forget about the joy of thrifting! Shopping at thrift stores or swapping items with friends is a great way to save money while being resourceful. It's also a wonderful way to teach your kids about sustainability and creativity. There's a certain thrill in finding something unique at a secondhand shop, and you can even make it a fun family outing. You're not just saving money; you're building a culture of creativity and conscious living, which will benefit your family for years to come.

Being debt-free doesn't just mean more room in your budget; it means more room for happiness, creativity, and quality time. It's about making intentional choices that bring you closer to your goals and your family. With a little creativity and teamwork, you can create a life that feels fulfilling and stress-free, no matter your income level. Living debt-free might take time and effort, but the journey is worth it—and it's a path that leads to a brighter, more joyful future for everyone.

Strategies for Paying Off Debt

Paying off debt can feel like a huge mountain to climb, but with the right mindset and a solid plan, it's totally doable. The first step is to get a clear picture of your finances. Write down all of your debts, including how much you owe, the interest rates, and what your monthly payments are. This will help you see exactly where you stand and help you decide which debts to tackle first. Focus on paying off high-interest debts because those cost you more in the long run. And remember, every little win counts! Paying off even a small debt is progress, and it'll keep you motivated to keep going.

Next, make a simple budget that works for your family. Start by listing all of your necessary expenses, like food, transportation, and household items. Then, take a look at where you can cut back. Maybe you can switch to store brands, plan meals to avoid wasting food, or find free ways to have fun together. Any extra money you save can go directly to paying off your debt.

You can even try out different strategies for paying off debt, like the snowball method (paying off smaller debts first for quick wins) or the avalanche method (tackling high-interest debts to save more money in the long run).

Involve your whole family in the process, too! Teaching your kids about money management can be a fun family project. Play budgeting games, or work on DIY projects that are cheap but rewarding. This way, your kids will learn valuable lessons about saving and spending wisely, and everyone will feel part of the journey. You can also get creative with low-cost activities—take walks, have game nights, or explore local parks—showing your kids that fun doesn't always come with a price tag.

Thrift shopping can also make a big difference in your budget. Turn it into a family outing by visiting local thrift stores or garage sales together. You can find clothes, toys, and home items at a fraction of the cost. Plus, it's a great way to teach your kids about recycling and reusing. You could set a small monthly budget for thrift shopping so you can stay on track with your debt but still have fun looking for great deals. Who knows what treasures you'll find! Every successful find can feel like a small victory in your debt-free journey.

Lastly, keep your focus on your long-term goals. Staying motivated can be tough, but remembering that every payment you make gets you one step closer to being debt-free can really help. Talk with your family about your progress and the benefits of being debt-free, like less stress and more savings for future trips or activities. Keep the conversation open and positive, and remind yourselves that you're all in this together. With patience, teamwork, and a little creativity, your family can beat debt and enjoy the freedom that comes with it!

Living Below Your Means

Living below your means is more than just a way to save money – it's a mindset that can truly change your family's life for the better. For families managing a tight budget or working to pay off debt, this approach offers a fresh perspective on how to make the most of what you have. It's all about focusing on what really matters, like quality time with your loved ones, creativity, and creating special moments without overspending.

One of the best things about living below your means is how it opens up fun, budget-friendly adventures. Family vacations don't have to be fancy or expensive. Why not try exploring local spots, going on a nature hike, or setting up a camping trip? These simpler adventures can be just as exciting, and they help your family bond while making lasting memories. You can also look for great deals on travel or use travel points to get discounts. Teaching your kids to enjoy experiences rather than expensive toys or outings helps them appreciate the little things in life.

When it comes to your home, DIY projects are an excellent way to stay creative while saving money. You don't need a huge budget to make your home feel special – just some imagination and a little effort. Repurpose old furniture, get creative with art from everyday items, or give a room a fresh look with a coat of paint. Working on these projects together as a family not only saves money but also gives everyone a chance to contribute and feel proud of the space you all share.

Cooking meals at home can also be a fun and rewarding experience that brings the family together. Meal planning on a budget doesn't have to be stressful – it can actually be enjoyable! Try batch cooking or using seasonal ingredients to save money, and get the kids involved by letting them help with chopping or stirring. You can even host a family cooking night where everyone contributes a dish. Not only will your family eat healthier, but you'll also teach your kids how to be resourceful in the kitchen, turning mealtime into a fun and educational activity.

Lastly, look for affordable ways to fill your days with joy and connection. Explore free community events, visit parks, or take a walk together in nature. Gardening can also be a great way to bond and enjoy the outdoors while teaching kids about patience and growth. And don't forget about the fun of a cozy family game night – no money required! Living below your means isn't about missing out; it's about finding happiness in the simple things and enjoying the moments you share as a family. By embracing this lifestyle, you can create a stable, joyful future for your family – one filled with love, laughter, and unforgettable memories.

Cultivating Gratitude and Mindfulness in Spending

Cultivating gratitude and mindfulness in how we spend can be a game-changer for families wanting to thrive on a budget. When we approach our finances with a mindset of gratitude and awareness, it changes the way we see money. Instead of focusing on what we don't have, we start to appreciate what we already do. This shift not only makes us feel happier but also helps us make more thoughtful decisions about our money. By being grateful for the small things, like a homemade meal or a cozy game night, we find joy in simple moments without overspending.

Mindful spending starts with awareness. Take some time to think about what really matters to your family. Is it creating memories together, having healthy meals, or making your home a welcoming space? When you focus your spending on what aligns with your family's values, it's easier to say no to things that don't matter as much. Involve your kids in this conversation, too! Ask them what makes them happy and what they value. This not only helps them feel part of the family's financial decisions but also teaches them how to make thoughtful choices about money as they grow.

Gratitude can also help guide your spending decisions. Instead of shopping to fill a gap, try appreciating all the wonderful things you already have. One fun way to practice this is by starting a family gratitude jar. Every week, each person can write down something they're thankful for. It's a small but powerful way to remind everyone of the abundance you already enjoy. This can make it easier to resist those tempting impulse buys or things that seem exciting at the moment but don't really bring lasting happiness.

Being mindful when shopping can actually be a lot of fun and feel rewarding, too. Before buying something, ask yourself: "Do I really need this? Will it make our family happy in the long run? Can we do this without spending money?" This kind of thinking can spark some creative solutions, like swapping clothes or toys with friends or finding cool items at local thrift stores. When you start approaching spending with intention, you'll find more ways to enjoy life's little pleasures without it costing a fortune.

As you work toward a debt-free mindset, gratitude and mindfulness will help keep you on track. Celebrate your small wins together, like paying off a bill or sticking to a budget. Share those victories as a family – it's a great way to support one another and stay motivated. When you focus on how far you've come instead of how much further you have to go, it builds confidence and optimism. By making thoughtful choices, your family can enjoy a fulfilling life, with stronger bonds and fewer financial worries. You'll see that living well and happily doesn't have to mean spending a lot.

Conclusion

Congratulations! You've made it through the guide to thriving on a dime. By now, you've discovered that living a full, joyful life on a budget isn't just possible – it can actually be a lot of fun! From creating meaningful family memories and enjoying affordable adventures to making smart spending choices and embracing a debt-free mindset, you've got all the tools you need to build a strong financial foundation for your family.

Remember, it's not about how much money you spend, but how much love, creativity, and resourcefulness you bring into your everyday life. Whether it's a weekend camping trip, a homemade meal, or simply spending quality time together, the moments that matter most are often the ones that don't cost a thing. Keep looking for ways to be resourceful, stay mindful with your money, and celebrate the small wins along the way. Your family's happiness doesn't have a price tag, and with a little planning and a lot of heart, you can continue to thrive – no matter your budget.

So here's to building lasting memories, creating joy in the little things, and living a fulfilling, debt-free life with your loved ones. The best adventures are yet to come!

www.ingramcontent.com/pod-product-compliance
Lightning Source LLC
Chambersburg PA
CBHW062225220526
45471CB00009B/3343